Sweet Betsy F1

Sweet Betsy From Pike

Stan Rogal

Wolsak and Wynn . Toronto

Copyright © Stan Rogal 1992
All rights reserved
No part of this book may be reproduced or transmitted in any form, by any means, electronic or mechanical, without permission in writing from the publisher, except by a reviewer who may quote brief passages in a review.

Many of these poems have appeared or will appear in *Probe Post* (ON), *Next Exit* (ON), *Green Fuse* (CA), *Carleton Arts Review* (ON), and *Skylark* (QC).
Thanks to the editors of these magazines.

Cover art: Jennifer McMackon
Author's photograph: Dave Rogal
Typeset in Palatino, printed in Canada by
The Coach House Press, Toronto.

The author thanks the City of Toronto and the Toronto Arts Council for their financial assistance toward the completion of this book. The publishers gratefully acknowledge support by The Canada Council and The Ontario Arts Council.

Wolsak and Wynn Publishers Ltd.
Don Mills Post Office Box 316
Don Mills, Ontario, Canada, M3C 2S7

Canadian Cataloguing in Publication Data
Rogal, Stan, 1950-
 Sweet Betsy From Pike

Poems.
ISBN 0-919897-28-2

I. Title.

PS8585.032S83 1992   C811'.54   C92-094095-1
PR9199.3.R63S83 1992

This book is for Robyn

The dynamic of evil is the attempt to make the world other than it is, to make it what it cannot be: a place free from accident, a place free from impurity, a place free from death.
- *Otto Rank*

CONTENTS

Yonder   13
Backwater   14
The wedge   15
Oracle   16
The wings of Daedalus   17
Fairy tale   18
Time, people, water, way, words   19
Rude alchemy   20
13 Ways of looking at a buckboard   21
Hobson's choice   24
Caliban   25
The pool of Salmacis   26
Pastorale   27
Interior landscape 1   28
Profile   30
Ciphers   31
Tourists   32
Paganini   33
The stone bed   34
Prime mover   35
Surf   36
Enigma   37
Imprimatur!   38
Labyrinth   40
Nowhere   42
Down the road   43
Lexicon   45
Crossing   46
Interior landscape 2   47
Branches   48
Owl   49
Bugs, snakes, and snow   50
The burning   52
Weather   53
The further shore   55
Grail hunters   56
Eldorado   57

Apologia   58
Fleur du mal   59
Dropsy   60
Constellations   62
The dig   63
Interior landscape 3   64
Breton's comment ...   65
Phoenix   66
Snow folk   67
Metamorphosis   68
Who knows   69
The river   70
Echoes   73
Comedians   74
Stars   75

SWEET BETSY FROM PIKE
(an American folk song)

Do you remember sweet Betsy from Pike?
Who crossed the wide mountains
with her husband Ike.
With two yoke of cattle
and one spotted hog
A tall Shanghai rooster
and an old yeller dog.

Sing, toor-a-lie, toor-a-lie, toor-a-lie-ay.
Sing, toor-a-lie, toor-a-lie, toor-a-lie-ay.

The ordeal of transformation, far from being a corruption, is an initiation and cannot end with the mere restoration of the earlier shape, or with anything short of the means for a new beginning.

- from *Metamorphosis: the Mind in Exile*
  by Harold Skulsky

YONDER

In the beginning was the wood.
Not here. Not this place. This city.
Whether Pike, Toronto (once known as York, and earlier,
   likely, named, unpronounceably/Native, and, before that,
     presumably, something, equally, Lethean)
Or an other.
Concrete.
Draining the skies
   and unbraining rivers with vain alchemy.
But yonder.
Such is the proposition, at any rate.
Who map distance a cure
   sets a course of no course
      placing fate in stars
  that may have blinked out
Centuries ago.
Never once entertaining
What goes around comes around
Moves civilization to wilderness
   packing the same old tools
      lugging the same awkward furniture
         mouthing the same empty promises
      singing the same boring songs
   bearing the same sad suspicion.
Prepared, as ever, to fire a bullet
Square
   between the eyes of the sphinx
      or spike a well
         deep
      to the heart of each
   hapless
Dinosaur
   journeys a people closer to zero
      further from X.

BACKWATER

Do you remember Sweet Betsy From Pike?
Crossing those wide mtns that were once.
MOUNTAINS.
There was a land. No less amazing
    for its naturalness.
But that was long ago and far away.
When dragons could be counted on
    to play their part. Smoking heroes
        from a green wood
            with enuf love to last
                Happy Ever After.
How quickly hero falls to horror
    when a generation sets its mind to dozing.
All those quiet woods.
Betrayed by the lumber of bored feet
    set seeking fame in the arms of Nelson.
Nowhere for a dragon worth its wick.
Not a hero.
Or even an ogre
    meant to frighten young children along the path.
Just Betsy. Shed of any liquid riot
    dulls an old saw against the grain.
Recalling:
    a dog
        a hog
            a home.

THE WEDGE

No highway, no tracks and flying
Unimagined.
Imagine them, then,
   toiling up the mountainside
      in a wagon drawn by two yoke of cattle.
Bound for the unknown
   and interrupted by the only likely crossroads.
Sky above, earth below.
Nothing but distance in the rear.
Ahead, the riddled wood poses:
   something occurs within this frame that is not neutral.
Without a traffic light to indicate procedure
Not one tree stands visible among all this forest.
No photographer can expect to record such absence.
In the face of it,
   a mind flushed with the beat
      of a thousand geese creates wilderness enuf
         to drive a tourist mad or swallow
      any delicate
   Alice
Whole.
No Alice.
Betsy. Sitting tall in the saddle
   not ½ knowing familiar shapes lose themselves
      among familiar surroundings.
A damp cigarette hanging from her cancered lip.
A hand on the reins, a hand on the axe
   and one eye on the camera.
Drives a wedge.
Deep.
To the heart of it.

ORACLE

When rowers row through dust
Tourists drop a coin and move on. What
    is the sense that translates phenomena to
Spectacle?
Unwilling to attend except from a distance
Alphabets a slate of criss-crossed lines
That would stake a vampire's heart
Let alone
These
Beat
Woods.
Such convoluted charm
Threatens each foreign tongue with stone
    and ignites forests
        with the polluted blood of ancient creatures.
Surely, on the lips of every fall hangs an oracle,
    yet, who would suffer transformation
        if the end result was change?
Tiresias touring the countryside
Sporting blank eyes, saggy breasts and
Enigmatic
Apples
Would have no better luck.
Nor a child wrapped in branches
Telling tales of nymphs
    disguised as lakes or flowers.
No maps. No guides.
Just the malignant course of stars
Unravelling this
Dumb-
Found
Nature.

THE WINGS OF DAEDALUS

Fallen hard upon. This place
Where even angels play it cool
Enflames a heart
    and fires a mortal's brain to wax.
A lifetime spent
Learning to draw a perfect free-hand circle
Creates some strange sense of
Heaven.
The pillars struck by a mere boy
    who bolts two iron arms in a loose joint
        and rings a conflagration
    that roasts a feathered uncle
To a turn.
Though this is false.
The angels false.
The flames false.
The feathers false.
Even the uncle false.
Unlike the concrete filling the tender skull
    and threatening to blink out the sun.
Or these wings
    fit only for beating a hollow whoop
        from the downy breast.
Who could have entranced gods with
    infinite convolutions
        ends scratching patterns in the dirt
    that molder
At the first rude heat.

FAIRY TALE

Once upon a time.
Well, you know how it goes.
There is an imperilled journey
    a puzzle to solve
        and everything happens in threes.
Kids forced to wait out the slow unwinding of stars
    shed their pink skins and learn to embrace the wilderness
        while adults grown crusty around the edges
    crumble into
Background.
Nothing more natural than this.
Death
That dissolves the borders
    between the self
        and the rest.

TIME, PEOPLE, WATER, WAY, WORDS
(the five most commonly used words in the English language)

People slaved one to the other content
With controlling the terms of their own unhappiness.

Barely kept afloat in this broke water
The trick that coaxes a snake from the blood, lost.

A time the first women died without a word
Firing brats as fodder to the wilderness.

Little joy in such expulsion
Giving up the ghost to a sky so full of holes
None could be counted on to lead a way.

RUDE ALCHEMY

Understandable, surely.
What other way to enter wilderness
   than armed to the tits?
Counting nothing there
   but bears, bugs, savages, and isolation
      scores every unimagined
   fire
Civilized.
No need to advance X
   with shields raised, swords drawn, visors down
      and conceits of endless fuel
         set to kindle gold from ashes.
Whether grass, toad, calf, or angel.
Given a snowball's chance in hell
Better
Than this religious
Fervour
Burning
   the more the supply the more the demand.
Its gorge wider by its very engorgement
   contents a people whose grasp exceeds its reach.

Time when words move less than water
   and water less than the altered blood of dinosaurs
      sparks a legacy of serpent's teeth
   spawning any new generation rooted in febrile muck
Brain-boiled.
Dragons
   too rude for woods
      that lash out at the first things that move
         (or don't)
Poison the water, smoke up the sky and choke the land
With sulphurous
Death.

THIRTEEN WAYS OF LOOKING AT A BUCKBOARD
(after Michael Redgrove's
Thirteen ways of looking at a blackboard
after Wallace Stevens'
Thirteen ways of looking at a blackbird)

i
Between one emptiness and another
The only unmoving thing
Is the wheel of the buckboard.

ii
Who are of no mind
Simply stone
In which there is one buckboard.

iii
The buckboard flapdragons in the wind
Under a guise of blue dust
It would wish itself apart.

iv
A woman and a man
Are none.
A woman and a man and a buckboard
Are fewer.

v
Why prefer?
There is beauty in emptiness
And emptiness in beauty.
There is the figure of the buckboard
And just after.

vi
A landscape crushed by ice
soon exhausts the summer
And vice versa.
The single thing the buckboard knows.

vii
O rude travellers
Ambitious for an untried land
Do you not observe how the buckboard
Spins straw to dust behind you?

viii
They have taught the lines on their hands
To foretell what they want to believe.
The pages of their books are filled with blue dust.
The buckboard (by turns)
Tells it differently.

ix
The buckboard eats its way
Tracing a curve of crumbs
So convoluted
No bird dares venture.

x
Whether it existed or not
No one praised the buckboard
Nor played the music
Grinding from its wheels.

xi
Turned from the face of it
Those mountains that slide to plains
Or forests burn to deserts
Too unreal, unlike, once, looking back
The shadow of the buckboard
Curried serpents from its hair.

xii
The river is drowning
The buckboard must be pissing.

xiii
The winter spent a year each afternoon
The summer spent the rest
Between the spokes of the wheel
The buckboard sat.

xiv
No fourteen
No buckboard.

HOBSON'S CHOICE

What other way to go but west?
East was in the past.
South was downhill.
To the north
   only fish, fog, and frozen tundra.

For folks hooked on *Once upon a time* ...
Beginnings
The offer of a second chance
   (most of 'em cast-offs, bankrupts, and criminals)
     with as much land as could be staked
       between sunrise and sunset
     on a summer's day
   ignited the vision
Once touched
   wilderness would fire to gold
     and horse piss steam to diamonds.

Fat chance.
Who are always able to make the worst
   of every good occasion end
     returning home
       their stomachs stoked with cinders
        their fingers burned
       their tongues a wag of blue ash
      their brains convulsed by snakes
Erupting way past stone.
Erupting way past any
Faint reflection.

CALIBAN

A stress of flesh against spirit
Deflowers
A race set to breed god's footprints.
So they say.
And so the divinity of the sexual act
Falls to
Fuck.
The lie that unshapes innocents
Wraps them in beaver fur
And has them clawing their own genitals
For craving pearls
Makes guilt a weapon
Preaching propagation should occur
In the same manner that sunlight gives water its sparkle:

w/o breaking the surface

Handcuffs tongues
And pillows heads with
Reptiles
Sparking icy flames that vision
Oysters turning to toads
And vice versa.
Sore afeared to cross the lion with the lily
Wishes stars to enter her as she sleeps
Swell her belly with a nest of clean, blue ash.
This still desire beside the rest
That longs to press a face coined in gold
Manages (barely)
To squeeze a Caliban from the
Slag.

THE POOL OF SALMACIS
    (cursed with the power to transform anyone
    into impotent half woman/half man)

No just reward when gods square off
    and the balance for one thing gained is another lost.
Ask any early dammed
    by an intercourse of snakes
        condemned to echo a footprint's image.
Or that first other
Hero-fell-to-horror
Hermaphrodite
    ending disembowelled and drowned
        at the hands of its maker.
Called up on the carpet to settle two fires
    each claiming the other hotter
        between the sheets
    makes
Deformity
    a botch
        when fear moves a body so far from the self
            snow packs the skull
        and a tongue had rather turn to ice than
Answer.
Who might have gained the gift of prophecy
    figured memory a mouse
        in the belly of a dinosaur
            in the gorge of a glacier
              in the crotch of a mountain
            in the womb of a planet
        in the egg of a universe
Uncoiled their eyes
    and pooled a juice
        of regenerative
Zero.

PASTORALE

Setting out to learn the tunes
   of all kind animal, bird, plant --
      even the rocks.

This wasn't them.

Sore afeared that behind each tree
   grows a second more powerful tree
      makes every unknown music
Suspect.
A wood of cries and whispers being no less dangerous
   that might drive a mind to rapture and entertain a fall
Boils this landscape prolific.
Where mud gives rise to mosquitoes and toads
   the rotting carcass of a horse generates wasps
      and the putrefying spinal cords of animals
Transform to snakes.
Crude sights for cruder eyes long riddled by the (s)word.
What underlies shapes and visions conjures further monsters.
The invisible. That certains death
   going hand-in-hand with knowledge
      outside the gate of any idyll garden.
Dammed against the rush.
Music so bare no hand could scale the distance
   head to crotch and remain
Untouched.
Dives for cover at the first strange utterance.

INTERIOR LANDSCAPE 1

Everything connected in this quiet floe.
Ice. That pinches in from the edge
   breaking water's symmetry with crystals
      and lining definite positions in some direction.
West, let's say.
Housing creatures thot to be
(for all the world)
Invented.
Landscape so chill
   one images a diet of
      algae, pollen and the ground bones of
   failed
gods.
From shrunken lips arise the propositions:
   Eat or be eaten.
   Kill or be killed.
Who'd've guessed the same after all this time.
Unwilling to embrace a single dragon
   without its legs cut out from under
      scores every journey
Hellish.
Advancing the notion of a course where
   vampires hang frostbitten from the limbs of trees
      birds freeze in mid-flight
         and children blow to snow
      drifting high above
   the roof tops
Readies every eye
   armed with picks, axes, shovels and
Dreadnoughts.

Who might dream ice castles and fairy gold
Instead.

Grow blue
Transforming shadows coiled 'round pleasant hills
    to ghostly snakes
        and riming trees with knife-wielding priests
        set to chop the heads
        off unsuspecting
    travellers.
Numb to any sense save this:
    Clapped in a swirl
    Neither fog nor mist
    The tongue retreats
    And deliberate teeth
    Clot the mouth
    With blood.

PROFILE

No
lack of
vision but so
strictly tunnelled
mountains
bore to
death
unsupporting
a single set of
prints
except as image
gracing
glossy travel guides
the thin shell
trembling
at the first
footfall
profile held
to be most perfect
buffaloes tourists
and trees
that might've stood
ten lifetimes
sink
to arse-wipe
for a
diarrhetic
dominion

CIPHERS

Tabula Rasa, she said.
Tabula Rasa, he said.
Though the neither of them had the slightest
Concept.
A rock, maybe, upon which to build.
Or an egg. Chockfull of any hungered thing.
Or the mouth of a child entrancing back to the garden.
Not this terrorain
Where substantial trees ghost into mist
And creatures crawl all moss and teeth from under stones.
A scape so elemental
Eyes long to exit the skull and root the seething muck.
Rolling from the concrete toward 'X' to create from scratch
Tears distance to crumbs even pigeons can't stomach.
No place for criss-crossed rowers
Meaning to print generations of noughts in this parenthetic
Heart.
Only the wilderness circling in on itself.
Diving to the bottom of no bottom and re-
Turning.

Tabula Rasa, she said.
Tabula Rasa, he said.
Though the both of them said
Nothing
Of the
Kind.

TOURISTS

Outlook dampened by a reign of wonder
Returns tourists to the cool comfort
Of the blue eye.
Away from sun and surf that merely serve to
Stimulate. Drinking beer from plastic cups nowhere
Nothing near this place.
Buggered up
With the five most common woods in the vernacular:
Time
People
Water
Way
Words
Contents a tongue
   that shies at the exotic.
The fact the fabulous can break through
   when an image is allowed to generate its own logic
     being reason a'plenty
   to pack a world into a shell of
Skulls
   no crash of sea can penetrate.
Why crave the real with such select footage?
Those young, tanned, nubile shadows
Screened in more-than-perfect living colour
Backed by tunes
Any body
   bent on applause might echo
     and not ever
   break
The surface.

PAGANINI

On days such as this.
Paganini on the radio
   when you don't want Paganini
      and changing stations only airs:
Paganini
   Paganini
      Paganini
Has you believing God does not play dice.
Easier than blowing dust from the mechanism
   or replacing a faulty dial, I suppose,
      though the none of this says nothing
   for the
Music.
Mystery always preferable when odds are stacked in favours.
Learned to overlook
   every mountain of pale bones
      that fails to tumble seven-come-eleven each which-way
   while children ante shoeless feet
And wind their play among convulsive skulls.
How much more freakish.
This unholy ghost that boxcars serpent's eyes
   for the price of footprints
Than this hand that passes cleanly through the wires
   fading tunes that never stand a chance
In ears bent double
Toward the
Cross.

THE STONE BED

Bitter fact is
Nothing much occurred
And little to converse outside
    weather, crops, and livestock made
A bore. Which invented sex.
Which bore
Further distance
And cabbage-eared children
Who bore
In their turn
And died.
What should have been
An act of
Love
Not what arose
Altered
Neither
    the moon's menstruating course
        nor the pulsive tide of history
Only these settled hearts
Fed on stones
Bored.

PRIME MOVER

There. Out there.
The same content.
The form, though,
Shifts.
Accommodating some
Physical
Necessity.
Like, the goddamn mountain
Boils
Into the sea
   and you wanna say:

It chose

This is one weird
Translation, or,
Failing that,
Fucking
Dynamite
The sum-
Bitch.

SURF

Not to mean. Precisely.
But to be-
Come.
Too becoming. This land.
Swelled with swell surf.
The skin riots. The skin quakes.
And the settled ghosts of settlers
    threaten to slip between the boards.
A point where the plain
   erupts mountains
      or sinks into a hole.
Music
All the moon's machinery
Cannot affect
That causes mud to hiss
Trees to dance
Rocks to sing
Birds & animals to exchange faces
And the clapped skull
      to tintinnabulate
Revolts.

ENIGMA

To remind you not to think of X.
Fails. Without its bones
   dragged rattling from the closet.
The mere skin enuf to strike a match.
Blazing at the window.
Great Catherine, fer instance.
Strapped to the belly of a stallion
   commands some deathless weight
      no am't of museums can hope to exhume.
Or Turing, early praised for dealing death to enigma
   suffers the charge of two assholes
      and a scrotum full of poisoned apple.
Or Betsy, propelled by a cloven hoof
   crosses the Fraser with a vengeance
      birthing a multitude of fish floating
Belly-up in her wake.

   Increasing strange. Humanity's
     sport with self-extinction. A thot
       no dinosaur could muster in 140 million years.

Forgetting what goes around comes around
Makes poetry a sugar tit
Without recognizing this wood is all middles
No one never ever getting no nearer than this
No one never ever getting no further than this
Advances
X

IMPRIMATUR!
(Nature and Letters have a natural
antipathy - *Virginia Woolf*)

The real world does not exist. Does not exist.
Though it tries. O, how it tries.
Not the way an egg tries to be a chicken
Or an acorn an oak tree.
But otherly.
Like a rock-pile tries to be a message.
That way.
Or an alphabet of geese.
That way.
Or a wood only children dare entrance.
That way.
A printed beach. A track of stars.
The impression ice leaves on a mountain face.

Lead to the margin and no further
Characters
    crusted in centuries' black blood
        no claw can scratch
    no water can disinfect nor
Discourse
Stamps
    a garden to dust and ashes.
The earth groans.
Trees shave their heads and scream.
Grass and leaves lament.
Birds, animals, insects, lizards, and fish wail.
Stones weep and beat their breasts.

Cries fallen on no ears not devilled in type
   that figure
      how much more oxymoronic it seems
   than the pond's mouth
Stopped
   by Thoreau's Pencil Factory
This
Unsound
Land-
Scape's
Strained
Recomposition.

LABYRINTH
Post coitum omne animal triste
After coition every animal is sad

When someone shouts his love to you
Sew up his lips.
Too long desired. This buss
   that leads nowhere
And keeps every maid struck tragic.
Unconvinced that repetition recollects forward
Attraction to a man whose size
   travels elbow to knuckle and no further
      strikes as Greek
   without benefit of
Fortune.
A volley of Eros winging hand-over-hand
(from somewhere well below the heart)
Insisting:
   No young woman should remain single
   lest she turn to vinegar
      (No less a lie than a man is not a man
      who retires his ship to a single snug harbour,
      though lacking the fire power of the age.)
Wraps a body in weathered threads
   willing enuf to be dragged backward
      through the asshole of the Minotaur
         for a promise of unrelenting light
      and a view
   of the
Ocean.
The Pacific. With its dense blue.
Entrancing
   a labyrinth like no other.

Certainly not that trip between her legs a man might take
    and come out the other side some little altered, but,
Otherwise.
That pares a hero to a pygmy
    with a boxing glove head, flippered arms
        and an erection for a fishing pole
Breaks in fits against the rocks
Reeling with the impression, here,
    the blood of monsters festers further monsters.
And here, Betsy, grown sick with the taste of amputated love
Cuts the strings
And kills.

NOWHERE
    (Cruelty becomes a habit when butchery is
    adopted as a means to pleasure - *Sextius*)

Nowhere translates *now here*
  when dozers level the final mountain
    for a view of ocean
  and increased land
Value.
Entranced by music meant to worm the dead
The living decompose.
Surely, every age reeks catastrophe
  and seems no place to bring a child, yet,
    the signs are never clearer:

    ANY HOPEFUL REDEEMER TIPPING
    TOLEDO AT 7 LBS., 8 OZS., WILL
    HAVE ITS WINKLE LOPPED BEFORE
    IT COMES TO HARM. (By order of ...)

In light of a journey that promised
  change enuf to restore
    a body
  to its
Self
Progress marks its passage
  in the blood of all kind animal.
Faced with a glut of builders
Demanding woods they fail to comprehend
  in any form outside this pale erection.
Employment.
Paves a brain
  and stuffs a mouth with pencil shavings.
Darknesses no candle burning in the heart
  can transform
Nor subtract.

DOWN THE ROAD

This was like long before Kerouac cut a rug across concrete
Ah-mer-ika
Drivin' nowhere to noplace & not carin' one way or the other
Just movin' that was the thing jump in the car & boot it
Goin' half-fast 'n fast 'n faster blowin' image to a groove
Downin' pints 'n quarts 'n poppin' bullets shootin' horse snortin'
Tokin' talkin' screwin' like there was no yesterday no tomorrow
No even today only the music rubber coverin' asphalt an eternity
Like these other two too expecting to trip the Light Fantastic
On zebra back measurin' tunes that might bring tears for years
Teasing some kind of bebop life from the uniformed bark
Wailin' let us wander you & I ...
Among the blue dust & busted stones & bones
Among the broken black water & shivered timbers
Among the entrailed pitch of dead & dying creatures
Among the shattered scattered tiger eggs & horsefeathers
Among the fulminated skulls of vampires
Among the white-washed fences almost sunk beneath the sod
Among the parched pumps & skeletal barns & houses
Among the tortured limbs of forgotten machinery
Among the blown tires & abandoned rusted wrecks
Among the acred mounds of green garbage bags & rotting grub
Among the tossed tin cans & caps & broken glass & styro cups
Among the pulp & paper mills & blast furnaces & foundries
Among the abattoirs & dog food factories
Among the plants that manufacture day-glo power & chemical
　death
Among the smokestacks & sewage pipes that lead to nothing
Among the derricks gas bars & automobile manufacturers that
　exhaust
Among the coca-colaed billboards & burger joints that infest
　this effluent plain
Among the wrappers baggers & packagers

Among the chop-sueyed french-fried cold-cocked towns & cities
    that nest & belch & fart & shit at the edges of porcelain-
    lined lakes & rivers & ever-thinning streams of mocking
    urbane unconsciousness
Among the idle chat & yak & fume & bluster
Among the quiet indignation & outrage & who-gives-a-fuck
Among the movers & shakers & down-&-outers
Among the tourists with their full bellies & empty sky faces
Among everything & everyone that could or should or might be
    traced
        along a mainline of crude petroleum
           & never once having or wanting to look back
                over the shoulder
Gaze into the rear-view mirror & recognize that grand old dam
    up to her pampered ass in crap
        spiralling down the toilet
    & dragging everything else along
With her.

LEXICON

An eye is done in a wink while a mouth goes on forever.
Nothing/no one prepares for this departure.
Oh, the tickets are bought or the gas tank is filled.
The bags are packed. There's a note for the paper boy
    and someone to water the plants.
But — this is not what is meant.
An eye. A mouth.
That thing out there that calls itself a world
    then suddenly changes shape.
No hog in nun's habit
    w/o a need to move past zebra
        translates this bark
    beyond the
Rude.
Time way gone when words are coaxed
    from the blood of people by a trick of water.
A five-fold kiss that proves.
Dead below the waist.
Securing a generation of fine
    fodder set square against the land
        that renders every paradise
Artificial.

CROSSING

When a little girl crosses over
It is called Oz. Or Wonderland. Also
Hell.
Who would not wonder in these odd woods
    nor entertain a music not rapt in snakes
        rocks the child from the branches
    dismembers its voice
And stuffs its mouth with bitter
Apple.
Slipped
   deep
      beneath the crust.
Eurydice.
Betsy.
Or an other
Once-bit-twice-shy
Blood-
Shed.

INTERIOR LANDSCAPE 2
(improvisation on a line by W.C. Williams)

Rather the ice than their way.
To take what is by single strength
   (theirs)
      in hands whose lines are trained
   to foretell
Nothing
Short of dominion.
Who seek a name that yawns eternal
Are unmoved by choirs of green-haired girls
   meant to lead travellers to misty river banks
Or music piped from barkish boys
   that tunes an ear to water.
Orpheus would stand no better chance.
Glancing back over his shoulder.
Struck dumb by bloodied ribs
   torn from slaughtered oxen.
Struck dumb by hearts
   so full of reasoned snow
      that feel little wonder for the new
         save to bugger seething ground
      with cold patterns of beets and spuds
   arranged to settle an entire wilderness
Incidental.
Straining counter to the flow
   riddles the possibility
      skin deep is as far as it goes.
Fine, until the old earth booms
   and shatters every frozen tongue to powder.
Struck dumb beneath the pitch
They vanish. They become
Woods
   you read about.

BRANCHES

No difficulty invoking a peaceful country.
Scene. Simply include
   the songs of birds in the background.
Hear them. Chirping between the branches
We casually call
A text.
The little bastards chirping
                      chirping
     chirping
 chirping
                chirping
For all they're worth.
Chirping their poor hungry hearts out.
As if the mere mention
   provides enuf real perch
To set them
Singing
Their tiny asses off

Forever

OWL

Where bides the owl in all this game?
Almost lost beneath the earth.
As the howl of wolves ghosts the dark hills.
Or the egg balances on the frog's heels.
Almost lost.
This sense of wonder and awe
More satisfying
Figures
Who calls its own name
Goes unanswered
In this rough shape.
Betsy, Ike or every other
Mud.
With no device to bend light around a glass
And pose the image as it was. Merely,
Sinking deeper
Into enchanted ground
Any body remains
Accidental.

BUGS, SNAKES, AND SNOW

In the movie
Molly Ringwald plays Betsy
And Tom Cruise plays Ike.
Amazing combination
    who earlier might have been Monroe and Mitchum.
The bugs are impressed.
The snakes are impressed.
Even the snow ends its swirly drift to take a peek.
Except, in the film,
    there are no bugs, no snakes, and no snow.
This having less to do with artistic license
    and everything to do with box office
        the bugs, snakes, and snow
            laugh up their sleeves, thinking,
Wouldn't Betsy and Ike have loved that?
Also, Molly and Tom are an extremely cute couple.
They wear cute prairie outfits.
They speak in cute Canadian accents.
The dirt on their hands and faces is cute.
They have a cute dog
    and the wagon is drawn by two real cute horses.
Where are them dumb oxen? wonder the bugs.
Where's that Shanghai rooster? wonder the snakes.
Where's that spotted hog? wonders the snow.
That's not all.
Molly and Tom discuss everything together.
In one scene Molly saves the life of the Indian Chief's son.
In another scene Tom cries.
This is a very progressive movie.
In the sex scenes Tom is always shown in underwear.
The underwear is clean and Tom (we notice)
    (almost naked) is, really, too cute for words.

Molly, also, is, really, too cute for words.
Her breasts, bare, are the perfect size and shape.
Not too big, not too small and so
    well behaved. Her nipples,
        perky, without being obnoxious,
    strike a fine family-viewing line between the
Erotic and the pornographic.
Someone has done their homework
    and the lovemaking scenes are quite honestly
        cute beyond measure.
Naturally, they arrive on the West Coast
None the worse for wear
    and proceed to amass a fortune
        selling lumber to the Brits
    to build ships
So that Nelson can defeat Napoleon.
The final shot is the presentation of medals
    against a painted backdrop of giant pines
        while the bugs, snakes, and snow
            split a gut off-stage
        rolling among the
    stumps, slash, and
Ashes.
Cute, they think. *Very cute!*
Who'd've thunk
A comedy?
And that's the end of the movie.
That's the end of
It.

THE BURNING

    i
There is a law against it. Naturally.
Fulminating in public.
For no good reason.

    ii
No direction without electricity
This one breathed fire.
Cloaked in fantastic wings. Desires
Not to slay dragons, but embrace
Dragons.

    iii
For hours watching salamanders
Shuffle in and out of flames.
Later, dreaming hyenas
Burning beneath her flesh.

    iv
That stars would ravish her while she slept
Then to wake
Pregnant
    with heat and dust. Alone.

    v
Phoenix aroused
Where once the ache was ice.
And in place of a belly, the belly's place.
This thought, too, fevered her mind
    and set her teeth to roost in Ike's cooling
Ashes.

WEATHER

Here. Where there exists
A margin of terror.
The weather. Suddenly.
Snaps.
And the lettuce planted
April 7
Freezes
April 27.
Rough
In this bush
That fails
Expectation.
The single constant
Being
Revision
Makes
Second nature
A bust.
Like concern
For angles
Balanced on a pin's head
Petrifies
As a fish drowns
Discovering
Water
Or a dinosaur
Tuned to ice
Quits
Its dumb play
And vanishes
From the block.

Or snow
Informed
By the warp and woof
Of unimagined
Creatures
Sniffs out
Entrance
To skulls
Long since
Given up
The ghost.
Poor bastards.
Shaken
To the very leaf.
The very root.
Sucked dry
And ground
To shadows
Across
The drift.

THE FURTHER SHORE

On one shore of the Lethe River
    (Did I say, "Lethe"? I meant, of course,
    THE SASKATCHEWAN [though, the difference is, really,
    Unremarkable.])

On one shore
    (The east, surely)
Of the Saskatchewan River
Desert, pale and cold
    (Where nothing exists
    But naked killing and corpse eating)
Bloodless footprints
Bent beneath the weight of fathers'
    (and fathers' fathers'
    and fathers' fathers' fathers' ...)
Bones
Collect water in broken pails.

Them
At first glance seeming
Unlike these other two in every way.
Betsy and Ike glowing in cloaks of luminous blue dust
Convinced
    once navigated
        there was anything an appetite could wish for.
Anything under the sun.

Discounting that (those) previous river (rivers)
Cursed by a foul century's blood
Polluted Betsy's waist with a whelp of chancres
    and Ike's teeth with a stomach for moldering flesh
        sets a course between them
Shades dare not
Cross.

GRAIL HUNTERS

An intact cup upon a table
Being
   a state of high order
      tends toward a fall.
This is only natural and
   what can go wrong
Will.
Whether Lancelot, Cortez
   or a couple bent on simple husbandry.
Bridges burned in the distance reappear
   grown out of proportion in this wood
      while the spilled guts of all kind animal
Evidence
      where people go disease follows.
At the edge of this
   a plank offers some mysterious promise.
Stretched above the dark
Moving
Water.
Space enough for a pair of armoured feet
   at peace with dragons (nothing more)
      buckles beneath the baggage
Thot
   to secure a world.
Answers any cup could riddle
   where a single rough question
      might tumble walls.
The path open.
The way clear.

ELDORADO

Amazed
In the footprints
Of a maimed Spaniard
They, too, set the ships burning
For
No retreat. This harbour
   that virtually flickered then
Sank
Them heading inland
Sniffing out savage gold.
What chance for a country lacking windmills?
Real swords ripe for the blood
Of real flesh.
Not Spain. Not Mexico.
Canada.
At this juncture motion ceases without a hinge to flex.
These same empty faces kept apart
By the same unholy grail
   any bat of the eye would
Alter.
No bat. Only vampires
Crossed
   beneath this black sun.
Them sinking deeper and deeper.
Too long at it
They mistake one wood for another.
Mud becomes blood
and their own dried turds
   haunt
      with the likeness of
Apples.
No more to shake the pillars from their spots
This conceit that falls to ash
Finds room in the smallest corner of an urn.

APOLOGIA

Framed
by woods.
Betsy and Ike.
Who could've been any other except for this.
Damned compulsion to name.
As if a handle might provide some guarantees.
That *Shanghai rooster* set to crow every a.m.
    or a scent to be nosed out forever
        by an *old yeller dog.*
Spermed by the severed balls of Uranus
    and sprung gigantic from the ground.
Gravity roots firmly in the brain
Trimming vocabulary to what is necessary
    to get along.
Where vampires hung from every tree branch
    burn unrecognized and a glass grown thick with bones,
        dragon flies and the tresses of drowned mermaids
    lie buried beneath the rut of
wagon wheels.
A settler's job being to settle.
Hacks one tough wood after another.
Levelling ground for a *hog's* paradise
    gorged on dull rows of turnips, beets, potatoes
        and endless acres of
    Golden
Silence.
For tongues tied to *two yoke of cattle* there is
    little else to do but
Follow.

FLEUR DU MAL

Not that there isn't to be found
Things beautiful.
There are. Only too much so.
More than enough
    to turn a brain to lake water
        full of sleek fish that move so quick
    no bait, no hook
Can touch 'em.
Here is the danger.
That makes every face
A sky
One wants to crawl
Inside
    and count the stars.
But even less.
The threat a single tree
Fingers in the bone.
Or a rock.
Or what goes on
Within the petals
Of a rose.
Or a fly.
With blue dust
Sprinkled
On its ass.
Pressed to figure
Nothing is
What it seems
Questions even this
Disguise of flesh
    that longs
        to root the earth and sprout
    its own crown of laurel
Leaves.

DROPSY
(A pathological accumulation of serous fluid in cellular tissue as in some body cavity)

The flood subsides
   and maybe the monsoon has passed.
No more dreaming smoky ghosts
   wailing in the chimney, or vampires
      fogging windows with their hot breath.
Now the real terrors begin.
Having to step outside the skull
   with no blue dust
      to charm
   a lie of liquid land
Inactive.
Rather knowing
Nature draws on some shapes to mend others
Images a scape of infinite im-
Possibility.
In a dawn hung with pregnant dew
   and the five-lipped Fraser shrunk back to its source
     the weed-grown swamps swell with life
       half-mud, half-flesh
     while tremendous stems sprout from fissures
   transfiguring mountains to the forms of beasts
One expects to breathe, stretch, stand
   and hunker off into the distance.
Blind hope some prophet
   whose embryo is a clod
     in this ploughed field
   will re-print the wood, finally,
Stable.
Up to their asses in it
Each shovelful threatens with creatures
   set to shed their molten skins
     and suddenly wing into the air.

Where a head
   buried in shit
      might provide a cure
   a footprint
Drowns
And the succulent tongue
Barks
   against a creep
      of leafy growth
         welling
      in the
Throat.

CONSTELLATIONS

Where the line breaks.
Is nothing.
Short of.
Ground.
By the mechanical moon.
These trees.
That sweep the stars' feet.
And stars that blind with their flagrant.
Inevitability.
Not quite elemental. Automatic.
A simple shape.
Obscures.
The rest.
Them sleeping face-up.
The yellow horns twisting deep.
Into the skulls.
Or a dreadnought.
Of blue dust.
Gone. Gone way over the edge.
Ike muffled in fangs and fur.
Betsy wandering the black space
   brilliant
      in a cloak of sea-serpent scales.
A child perched in branches connecting dots.
Mouthing exotic, oh!
Names:
      Corona Borealis.
      Serpens.
      Libra.
      Ursa Major.
      Andromeda.
      Etc.
      Etc.
      Etc.

THE DIG

Digging deep into the bone.
No word of the wild
   from jaws that hack wood
      out of sheer employment.
Even admitting Thoreau's Pencil Factory
Must've played a part
Forgets the artificial.
Once upon a time composing
Woods devoid of 'skeeters, flies
   and every other biting
Ice
      that now stands poisoned beside the rest.
Diving straight to the heart of every bird
   drunk on moonlight.
This is the draw that water has.
Then pulls the ground out from under
   when the roots give up their hold.
The eye failing to contain the grand picture.
Clings to the rim of a plastic blue bucket
   while a whole ocean
      fades to
Nowhere.

INTERIOR LANDSCAPE 3

Sharp contours and merciless light.
Sky
Shot with skulls
Moon
Swelled with barking dogs
Bare
Yellow teeth
Over dark waters
Oily-skinned
Trees
   (birch, pine, dogwood,
   Douglas fir ...)
Transgressed by ice
Seeming
For all the world
Empty
Cartridges
Land
Buried in snow
The house
The house
Barely visible
Behind smoke
   (screens, locks, curtains,
   dreadnoughts ...)
And the single
Haunting sound
The feet
Of the hanged
Man
Knocking
Knocking
Knocking

BRETON'S COMMENT THAT VALERY
WOULD NEVER PERMIT HIMSELF TO WRITE,
THE MARQUISE WENT OUT AT FIVE

Then *what*?
Even admitting woods unnecessary once spooked,
   yet, first, they must be spooken, no?
The wise-acre who sez:
     "The longest journey begins with the first step."
All them wise-acres.
Remember?
With all that other shit we were meant to swallow.
Like:
     "Today is the first day of the rest of your life."
And:
     "God helps those that help themselves."
Jars, rather knowing,
   when a door is not, (suddenly), a door. Or,
     how get down off an elephant.
This haunt
Framed
By dumb ghosts
And dumber jokes
   goes way over the heads
     disfiguring branches to the shapes of beasts
   that rub their fur against the door.
Them wise-acres
Unimpressed.
Their baggage packed and ready
   for the annual flight to Capistrano.
The lights out.
The cab in the driveway.
The key in the dead-bolt.
The hasty note that reads:
     Betsy and Ike went out at five.

PHOENIX

What follows.
Moving one darkness to the next
Smokes out any landscape over-impressed with woods.
History has it. Twisted
    at the ends and blown three sheets to the wind.
Not knowing where to go but in a hurry to get there
    arrives nowhere near the edge after so much distance.
Believing a trail of clods and ashes ingredient enuf
    to spring a race of giants
        trims vocabulary to the bone.
Gloom no Phoenix bent on fire
    can expect to subtract given
Endless
Generations.

SNOW FOLK

A trip fuelled by rumours of the fantastic
Overlooks the real.
Landscape stretched from sea to sea.
So open an eye could roll forever
    and still remain on centre.
The fear that keeps a tourist mistaking the invisible.
Loaded for dragon where there are no dragons
Blows a wood to smithereens
    for the price of a toothpick
        and a crop of mean potatoes.
Making plain. Between composing poetry and
    a railroad there is no common ground
        for these kind folk content to melting.
Blank to all purpose save what remains.
At either end of this phoney rainbow
Mounds of trash and debris put on their ugly faces
Freezing birds in mid-flight
    and transforming lions
        to stone.

METAMORPHOSIS
    (Though all things change,
    nothing is destroyed - *Ovid*)

Who would remember?
Faced with trees of such convolution
    birds that fly to roost
        die lost among the branches
            and rivers swirl with powers
      to unwind brains
    into nets of radiant
Fish
Who could?
This forest seemingly
Unbound
Unfathomable
Heat
That alters every living thing.
In the ancient pattern
    a hero's homecoming ends
        in recognition. But, what about the
Other?
The handsome youth struck with horns and hooves
    then disembowelled by his own faithful dogs?
The beautiful maiden fleshed with bark
    and sprouting bouquets of laurel leaves
        from her ears and throat?
Or even the plain and simple
Disfigured
    through centuries' rooting earth and ashes?
Brought to bear in these bare woods
No gardener has been known to die
In the memory of a
Rose
Figures
Who should?

WHO KNOWS

And (who knows), perhaps there is (like
   so much else in this fishbowl space)
A limit to the am't of violence
A world can contain.

And (who knows), perhaps tomorrow (or
   the day after or the day after that)
We somehow must return
Within the fold of Paradise.

Though (who knows), perhaps this means (and
   will it then, be worth it?)
A cosy spot for two, alone.
A he. A she. Not us.

A serious (who knows), perhaps consideration (but
   can it really be?)
A universe begun with a bang
   and ending with its head stuck up its ass
      that traps God in the branches of a tree
         forced to play out the same tired cards
           hand
               after
                hand
                   after
          hand
            after
          hand
            after
              hand
                after
              hand

               .
               .
               .

THE RIVER

      i
Betsy dreams she is a river.
Not any river. *Every* river.
        Nile. Ganges. Tigris-Euphrates. Amazon.
        Yangtze. Mississippi. Snake. Even the
        Fraser.
No mean feat
   and paints herself:
Cold
Blue
Pure
Glacial
Being her idea of the perfect river
Everything else arises out of her.
Sharing in all she is a part of nothing
   and to link earth with the stars she considers
Contentment.
Then advance the people
   and black reign falls across the land.
The very beautiful die first: unicorn, dragon, griffin.
Nymphs shed their fair disguise of bark and leaves
Spilling guts that writhe and twist into
   mad shapes
      of bloodied human faces.
Unripe demigods shake from tree branches
   and smash their skulls upon the jagged rocks.
The great forests hack to ships and base metals bend to
                            weapons.
Even the wise and artful cannot endure.
Sphinx crumbles.
Tiresias gorges and chokes on a diet of wormed apple.
Orpheus explodes
   scattering his pieces to the deaf wind
      until no trace remains but

  Death's straining
Rattle.
The land itself loses its tongue and takes to frets and
              gutterings.
The shrike presides. Butcher bird
  who charges life with death and death with life.
One thing food for another in this plagued space
  that fills without
Fulfilling.
And rats. Eating holes in the bellies of swine
  chewing the elephant's feet
    nibbling the ears and toes of infants
  breeding utter
Destruction.
Betsy spreading her arms and cradling what she can
There seeming no end
  to debris, spoil, and entrails.
Centaurs wash their wounds and needle her veins with
              poisons.
Spines of the dead transform to snakes
  and snakes' teeth usher further generations
    of corpse-eaters.
Fire bites deeply into the terrain, the soil,
  for it is flammable. Smoke becomes a way of life
    and from the soot and ash spring villages, towns, cities
      with ability to reproduce
    from their own
  foul
Waste.
Now the river, hanging dark and heavy in her bed,
  turns in upon herself and disgorges her freight.
Tons of trout and salmon breaking the surface
Belly-up
Oxygen-starved or blistered or malformed beyond enduring.

Too many for any amount of preying
Vulture
    or heron meant to devour and eliminate.
Betsy grown thick, ponderous in her journey to the sea.
Pitched with the pregnancy of a dinosaur.
Water
That refuses to break
    against the salty tide. Her bulk merely
        sliding beneath the waves
            colliding with untold other
                ill-considered rivers whose bodies
            weld
        creating some hitherto
    Unknown
Multi-headed monster
    soon to emerge
        erupt
            and shroud the world
        in its cloudy
Wings.

    ii
Awake. Betsy walks outside, sees the river
    sparkling in the sun. Its waters
        packed with fat, ripe fish
            the banks steeped with timber
                the fields flooded with rich, golden wheat.
"Never," she shrugs.
"Never in a million years."
Her turning, raising the rifle
    and firing into the branches of a tree.
A mewl.
Rapt in crow feathers.
Silenced.

ECHOES
> (For whenever a thing changes and quits its proper
> limits, at once this change of state is the death
> of that which was before - *Lucretius*)

Tangled in the eyebrows of the mountains
Unbrains
   when snow swirls visions even dogs can't shake.
Amazing woods
Spooked
   with the twisted shapes of creatures
      that moan and groan and cry and could other-
         wise be people
   if not for so much
   damned
Rooting.
Fallen off the path as well.
Numb to the fact
Footprints end
   precisely where the eye craves entrance.
Base trees writhing up out of the muck.
Barking convolutions no skull remains unravished
Nor the voice
Disappearing
   leaf to leaf
      until "remember me" is just a ghost
         unallowed to step in from the cold
            longer than a feinted glimpse.
Echoes:
Remember me.
   Remember me.
      Remember ...

Who

COMEDIANS
(To perceive life as farce, travesty, and transformation is to be confronted by the comic mask of Isis - *Harold Skulsky*)

So howcum no one's laughing? I mean,
Where's your sense of humour in all this?
I mean, what the devil is this whole earth,
    with its sentimental companion the moon, good for,
        except to be
Mocked?
These good-adventure-folk
Far too real to be taken serious.
Who wear beards on their backsides
    and cover their genitals with phoney noses
        and dark glasses.
Who leave no turn unstoned
    yet, attack old people for eating soup
        in the old-fashioned way.
Chaplinesque, baby.
This concern for propriety.
Property.
Whereas it is the louse
    (having adapted itself to parasitism)
That attains the ideal of bourgeois
Civilization.
Plus ça change rien ne change, eh?
Beneath the grave-
Stone
Flesh
Riotous
Skull
Laughter.

STARS

The coast of B.C.
It's foggy.
The Pacific crashes.
Having arrived at the end
    and discovering everything the same
        in all directions.
Stars maintain their distance.
There. Out there.
Somewhere. Somewhere.
Somewhere
    out of reach.
When for so long they appeared
    brooched to the lapels of trees.
Diamonds to be plucked and eaten along with:
    apples, pears, peaches, plums,
Vampires.
Ghosting in the spray.
Intrusion of the unknown
    more delectable
        for its namelessness.
Listen.
In this place woods reflect
    the sounds of woods. Hear them.
Their hairy legs.
Rubbing together.
High above this water.
Atop this ledge.
Leaning toward these stars.
This sheer
Abandon-
Ment